**Scivias Choreomaniae is a danger to society.** It exposes cadavers hidden from days to decades ago—from the rotten skulls of doctors to the rotted bones of prophets the medical staff held captive in their madhouses. This is Lake Angela's dance to the death, and you must enjoy it, and you must heed the holy madness.

Georg Amsel, co-author of *Ein Seidennetz/*
*A Silken Net of Stars and Lice* with Lake Angela

**Lake Angela's *Scivias Choreomaniae*** is a necessary, impressive collection chock-full of holy visions and sharp beauty, of "horses [who] drink from the pouring wounds of night," "birds [who] cling to necks with stark feet and razor beaks," and "flowers [who] gleam scalpels through their golden eyes." This gorgeous and generous sharpness carries the pain of miscarriages and violence felt as a person who experiences life as multiple. Open the book and flip your world: see how decay is "a special kind of beauty;" the hawk, a savior; scorpion, a friend; serpent a creature of god, and the patients at the insane asylum where Lake stayed as a dance therapist—are prophets. At the asylum, you'll learn how to fly like a bird and dance rain as you "spill from your bodies." Magic lives in this book. *Scivias Choreomaniae* is a world cracked open with possibilities. Lake will convince you that cockroaches are mentors and in sleep we can "understand bird sign." Read these poems and you'll be forced to step out from the world you think you know. These poems are packed with the knowledge of multiple lifetimes.

Sara Ries Dziekonski, author of *Today's Specials*

**This is a book to satisfy those** who seek poetry from outside our familiar culture with all its assumptions and wants. Lake Angela brings a modern sensibility to her writing while drawing on the medieval way image and symbolism unite. Facing human issues common to all eras she has a ruthless mysticism and is unafraid to think in terms of the soul's struggle to survive. She is equally secure at the social fringe with its asylums and hospital wards, venturing to those for whom being understood is the first step to being healed. *Scivias Choreomaniae* is proof that the age of visions is still with us and helping us see beyond the obvious.

David Chorlton, author of *Speech Scroll*

# Scivias Choreomaniae

## Lake Angela

SPUYTEN DUYVIL
*New York City*

## Acknowledgments

*Another Chicago Magazine*: "My Room," "Stomach, God, Glove, and Fruit," and "Kind Darkness."
*Brainz Magazine*: "The Birth of Savior Hawk" and "Savior Hawk"
*Cholla Needles*: "Choreomania," "Remedium," "Burnt Yarrow," and "Patriarcha"
*filling Station*: "Pilgrimage" and "Prognosis"
*Great Lakes Review*: "Dragging the Lake" and "Walking Again at the Asylum"
*io Literary Journal*: "Dance Therapy"
*ONE ART*: "Restraint"
*Osmosis Press Featured Writing*: "Haruspex *Δ↔*"
*!Pa'lante!*: "Dance Therapy for the Patients at the Asylum"
*Paper Dragon*: "Scivias"
*Plainsongs*: "The Children"
*Please See Me*: "The Women's Waltz," "The Other World," and "The Doctors"
*Seneca Review*: "Votive"
*New York Quarterly*: "The Innocent"
*The Bitter Oleander Press*: "Hawk Reprise" and "Buttercups in a Bag Around the Neck"
*The Broadkill Review*: "Orthodoxy," "Genuflection," and
    "What People Say to Me When My Stomach Shrinks"
*The Closed Eye Open*: "Carbo Animalis"
*The Ocotillo Review*: "Heterodoxy"
*Thimble Literary Magazine*: "The Chaplain"

*For the patients at Osawatomie—*

*Scivias. Know the ways.*
    -Hildegard of Bingen


*Nulla e tutto...Tutte le confidenze inenarrabili, vedo con tanta tenebra. Nothing and everything...All the ineffable confidences I see with profound darkness.*
    -Angela of Foligno


*Die minne sol sin mortlich. Love should be fatal.*
    -Mechthild of Magdeburg


*I know you choreograph dead bodies.*
    -A, Dance Therapy Patient at the Asylum


*The psychotic drowns in the same waters in which the mystic swims in delight.*
    -Joseph Campbell

*Our unflickering source of fresh visions, the healers of wounds struck*
*by words, is a host of seers. Only context determines whether*
*the visionary is called mystic or psychotic: the former is presented*
*a Lake and the latter a drowning pit. The medieval death sentence*
*became hydrotherapy, the drowning remedy also a punishment.*

    Scivias Choreomaniae *is composed by our system of hosts*
*and others who swim and drown alike, from modern to medieval times.*
*We always have thrived in between—days, waters, silences, darknesses—*
*forming and unforming as we create, transforming the waters in our*
*wake.*

    -Lake Angela

# Contents

**III: Three Kinds of Madness**

# I:
# CHOREOMANIA

## VOTIVE

The figure of God's Mother appears to me
in plastic, in miniature. What does it mean
to be fleshless, to be permanent? To be
unable to bend or to move on your own.
Then the dog of fire kisses my eyes open.
His gentle tail betrays the Son of God unfolded:
multiplied; God was schizophrenic, like me,
multiple, like me. That was before God
was a man, when God still had a Mother.

# PROMISES

When you crack open a mirror and see
everything that never can be reflected,
the heart catches on a dream and clutches.

I have given birth to three dead children.

A sacred dog collected them in his jaws
and cared for them: safer to eat the small bodies
than to leave them under a layer of thin earth.

I look for the other half of the bloodstream
among the more hearts decomposing.
Sun dashed on ice grows weak as though bled.

One day we will have a yellow afternoon.

In the periphery, an intestine unfurls. Death
comes early when the people of the forearm
reach the strict capital of the heart.

I do not write poems anymore. I have lost
control of all canals, including the uterus
and the mouth. Another word writes me:

*Glory be to her, for under her robes I see nothing but God.*

## DELIVERANCE

Now that I've kissed your prayers, will you carry
the Bird of Love with you? I've lost control.

I noticed another intestine unfurl like a rug.
Death is early again. In the courtyard

where I was enclosed, Christ caressed me
with the stakes that forge the stigmata: off limits.

I hear the birds calling and crying outside.
They cannot enter. Hummingbird nailed to the rafters

by outstretched wings, the tiny sources of color and light,
is unaccustomed to feeling heavy, her head hung

under her crown. She is the new Bird of Sorrow.
My womb holds her holy ghost. I hope she will find

comfort there, that by my blood it becomes clear
sins have not existed.

# DESCENT

Here I sit, without any feet,
hand on a crucifix ready to fly.
Clutch my bloody rosary.

## ORTHODOXY

My first language, water, was driven
from me by steadfast threats of sulfur.
Guilt stares at me from my ghost, yellow
holes in the head, hands, feet.

The hermitess on the river's cleft lip
in her blue gown clean with mud
was hired as a beggar
and licensed to pray.

The long-separated souls of the mountain
lilies sing an antiphonal dirge for their bygone
petals. Faceless, the ghost rushes back
between my legs.

## HETERODOXY

What is delusion, though? God loves the hungry.
But the holy anorexic feels abandoned after eating

only God, her host. Every forty days, medications
are manufactured from the remnants of exertion.

And what if you drown in the song you are singing
because the palate is ice? Sense in the bloodstream

it is midnight on that earth and the winter streams
from semi-tortured mouths. Carry the evidence

in case you are questioned. Avoid the tunnel
of fatal sound sent out to find you. The left eye

twitches in the glaring light. Reenact your fall:
the moment you hit the cement you collapsed

into waves of ululating sinew, understanding grace.

## CROSS EXAMINED

My personal
persecutory delusions are ablaze.
Waters, polluted by a priest's words, become flame.
*Spiritus Sulphuris,*
so be it.

Later,
in her barren state
hospital room they adorn her muted frame
with pomegranate gore and golden ears of corn
as befit an empress
of the age.

Long ago,
stretched upon the rack, arched preposterously back,
demons in green hospital caps
tugged at the body's teeth
and toes.

For her feats
upon the cross God offers her the perfect draft:
hemlock, opium, and wolfbane.
Honey for the other
pains.

# CHOREOMANIA

Winter woke up in my eyes. The orange tree frosted over:
I was in Hell, a hole where my stomach had been, my uterus
a shuttle flown off but fallen, the faulty birds broken in three.

God said, turn three times to put them back together. But once
begun, I could not stop the momentum. I died of the dancing
sickness, the plague preserved in my eyes among ice crystals.

Snow angels begin to rot; black clots slide down their thighs
and turn to hearts. The faceless man is trying to kill me again.
Winter clears my vision: I suspect my sometimes lover, God.

## Remedium

Every morning I find the resurrection incomplete—a bird
I cannot reach. Nor can I pull the thorns from her wings
or soothe her with my blood when she weeps. Both
my hands were cut off, hung with the herbs, and dried.
They stand twisted on the wooden shelf with hanged
yarrow and the hoop warped from woodbine.

## Patriarcha

Now I have more memories than I can hold.
Did I really see myself crucified, afloat
on the wave? Travelers try to hide their breath
from me, afraid in my alliance with Lake

I can read the shape of any water. Our fathers
lost us in a place denuded of colors. They remain
behind hidden walls, fingernails scraping bloody
stone as they count with eyes closed. We are far

from our proper desert. We wander and seek
a sister in trembling black robe made of mosquitos.
She wears the living robe to atone for her flight—
yes, her ability to survive, too high, too far.

She even emanates the color black, though it lives
on her blood, and she itches from foot to crown,
unable to scratch. No one may touch. We will be
the fathers—perhaps no better—to ourselves alone.

## What People Say to Me When My Stomach Shrinks

It's for the best—you'd lose the baby anyway because you are multiple.

Why did you believe you could continue to dance? Did you also leap?

You must not be quite strong enough. Maybe your vagina is weak.

This is the consequence of using birth control before. Maybe God

doesn't want you to be a parent. Everything happens for a reason:

maybe this is your punishment; maybe it is a trial. It is irresponsible

of you to choose not to eat other creatures when your babies needed

your meat; life is about more than just you, you know. It was God's will.

Was the miscarriage elective? You carried it wrong. At least you carried

it longer this time. It's probably for the best—you might have hurt

your children because schizoaffective people are violent. There was

probably something wrong with it, and it's better not to have a child

with Down syndrome or with conditions like yours. You can always

adopt; children in the foster system are troubled already. Maybe God

has other plans for you. You only had surgery on your uterus; you should

try harder. You can try again. Think of this as cleansing your system

for a real child.

## Pietà

Someone read me bedtime stories
of the black plague
and other-colored deaths,
and the water never turned away from us.

The words say what you make
from your pain matters:
black eyes, detached forest you can open
the moment you need to know you are
alive—or you can choose to love
the decayed corpse held in your arms
and know you too are dying.

But for now you still live,
so go on ascending. Your child
with eyes that never open
sits in the highest place, shining
obsolete from the golden throne.

Clutch the bouquet of henbane.

# GHETTO

I am afraid to enter the quarters in my brain where my banished
selves are kept, denied access to the view through the eyes.
They sense only scratches on pink, windowless walls. Held
by pressure, they are vacuumed, sealed, and cleansed, though
sometimes one is strong enough to break past the pulpy
walls, bloody shreds dripping from the hands outstretched.

One is a skeleton of a woman, hair torn and dirt-caked. One
drapes over a nest of layered blood: crust-congealed placentas
reeking of better progeny. One is an old man, gentle without
his memory. All are restless, tortured by cold, the isolation
chambers, the wrongly tinted light as it falls outside this world.

Cockroaches care for the best of the rooms, quietly preserving
the bodies with strokes from their silken legs. Deep inside,
one child still breathes. Eyes wide, she sees through the ice
and in her small arms cradles half of a hawk.

# GATEKEEPER

The ants come warbling by. The ants deserve respect.
Fire red and gleaming black, the insects bear a flag.

Purple with poison brush: the royal crest. Yellow ants
swarm the nest, formic acid floods beaks and eyes.

The cockroach bears the drifting weight
of all the colors in blue. The prophet who slips

from my side through the blue smiling slit
tongues the bleeding truth behind the body.

She scuttles the code easily to her protector.
She moves the word in waves; she is the new gatekeeper.

The Queen is in her hidey hole watching the sweeter ants sleep.

# GENUFLECTION

Unable to balance them all in her own opened arms,
the ghosts of birds cling to her neck with stark feet
and razor beaks. She trails her fear behind her,
and as she winds down each red corridor
leaves a little tremor in every cell, an eternal string
of softly genuflecting blood
that does not lead back.

She is the wordless poet with white feathered throat;
the quill crimsons her gullet to regurgitate
the wrong writing. Known by her Latin name,
Hippomane, the little apple that makes horses mad,
she draws the North American forest into being.
She weans the next savior on the poison secretions
of the blue otter, leaves him beneath the manchineel,
his mother's minor breast. Even the sap crackles,
blistering and blinding us.

The mother of all rises and resumes her journey.
Banished from too many worlds, she keeps silence,
yet echoes resound. They are the tantrums
and hunger pangs of the suckling God
left alone for this eternity.

—

In sleep I understand birdsign. When I wake I rise
to the dark, arching my back into the shape. Soon
I will enter the storm that stripped my stomach.
Segmented mind, soon I will be inside myself dying.

Asleep in the book, tempting the destructor, I outrun
a burning current back to the desert—always end
with an em dash, a knife. An escape to life O takes
shape M: only signs scattered at the foot of the nest.

Bring me your dreams wrapped in paper, dripping
with the undiscovered. Even as the dream desiccates,
my birds will read the signs. Black birds become
my eyes, and the solution is a worm in one iris.

## Haruspex *Δↄ*

The haruspex *Δↄ* is summoned
to read my entrail's omens,
the crows given a chance to translate

before the last sacrifice. >)))) >))))) >)))) A foreign
spark ^^^ ignites heaven's embassy windows.{0}{0}
Carrier pigeons (<>) blink in delight.

Fierce and terrorized, half »« dead
and holy ° inside my suppurating ```` wound. : > —
An errant wind whistles, cold flung along

stripped corridors \\ , spent nebula fingers ~~~~~
grasp nothing. A great cat ↕↕↕↕ shoots past:
all my memories thrash weakly ↜¦°↯\W/↝

in the vice {◁[◁]◁} of his jaws. Terrible green ⋈
stillness, a silence I cannot decipher. <((((( <((((( <(((((
The inchpin wound (∫∫∫∫) around the child's neck

puts my dreams to rest. ↝ ☉ ↜ Soon all will be
abolished: this whole world >))))
has been expressed.

# II:
# ASYLUMS

# Asylum

On the road I doze to the pitch and roll of my own deep
and different darknesses I do not yet fully comprehend.
My wound trails from the coast to the center, winding away
what the doctors dismissed as *products of conception.*
By the time we stop, I am empty
and more thoroughly exposed than I ever have been.

Our destination was a refuge built by Friends of the Mentally
Ill. Now that the inpatients have no friends, it is a prison
for those deemed not guilty of rape and murder by reason
of insanity. On the same wards the victims of torture
are huddled into corners. Those committed for associative thinking
or petty treason await judgement. I have come to heal with dance.

There is a bastion formed by stubblefields, valleys of horses
and hawks who escort me along the wires, and corroded metal
devices for retribution discarded along the hilltop fringed
with streams and memories that seep from condemned buildings
skirting the hospital that bore the title *Asylum for the Insane.*
I augur I am finally going home, a cold raw hope
I press between my palms.

# DANCE THERAPY FOR THE PATIENTS AT THE ASYLUM

Exempt from the trapdoors, the traps, the trapeze,
the sentenced, I am allowed to return to the cottage
of strange burials. In the grotto, the sun lowers weapons
like colors. Test with the feet while falling in; corridors
open into frozen fields with white, hawkless trees. One
ward in disuse awaits action from dancing dust particles
or the ghosts of birds who fly in and become trapped,
imprisoned a wall away from the men who raped autistic
and paraplegic children and tossed crumpled dollar bills
upon their naked shapes—except the sparrows do not
commit crimes and should not be remanded in solitary.
The patients' favorite dance is *flying like a bird*. Hands
gripping their girth, they jiggle to measure the weight
of their bellies and test the possibility now of flying off—
through the highest window, triple-paned, soundproof,
and untouchable.

## A Walk Outside the Asylum

You may choose not to listen to the disturbing
      frequency of the grey permeating this air, but it jars

your cells, carries you home. Through the drone
      of a minor key rain, the deserted courtyard, the forsaken

tuberculosis cottage emits white flames. No one
      is there to witness your correction. Security cleaves you

in two and banishes one of you from the body.
      The grey shadow of a patient pounds the smudged

safety glass of her cell, howls a Phrygian cloud. She can tell
      you are on the wrong side.

How will you choose? You do not have the privilege—
      because you want to live

                  out here, or anywhere.

## My Room

I am handed a key and commanded to walk
to the edge, where the asylum invades the field

of winter wheat. I find my office in an abandoned
cottage littered with past patients' last words:

the burst belly of a drum bleeding in the bathtub,
a rusted knife splitting the lip of the kitchen sink,

composition books recording blank yellowed pages,
a bird's clean skeleton bleaching on the sill.

Bare and dusty from preparing dance therapy,
my feet graze the surface of the forgotten cemetery.

Underneath the main grounds the morgue is numb
with preserved tongues and orbitoclasts for lobotomy.

Underneath my desk where I doze with the snake
who nests in my brain rest the bones of the hospital's

unnamed dead. It is disrespectful to sleep over the stones
of the insane without dreaming our dreams.

# THE CHILDREN

The asylum schoolhouse is long-locked but not empty:
on a child-sized desk a tattered doll holds a tea party
with a glass vial labeled *laudanum*. It was compassionate
to teach children who lacked the innate capacity for reason,
those more bestial than the cowed prisoners led to expend
their animal passions in orderly gardens: now a wilderness
crowned with violet-red musk thistle, the outlaw cousins
of sunflowers said to choke cattle to death. Bindweed cracks
window glass, unfurling soundless white bells. Johnson grass
breaks past derelict floorboards, ascends the dirt-caked
classroom's sundried silence.

                                                    K describes
her old school desk as though there is nothing remarkable
about growing up in the state asylum. Born in C Ward
to a silent reception among patients nodding like thistle
planted in metal chairs fused to brown floors, she never left.
From fellow students committed for idiocy or epilepsy,
she learned her first words. Tremulous scrawlings of horses
copied from picture books still adorn her open door. The farthest
she has traveled from the plastic mattress that has always
been hers is the graveyard beyond the quadruple set of doors.
Though the stones are marked only by numbers, she knows
which weights cover her childhood friends. I wonder if, like me,
she watches the bindweed climb and the yellow pigweed dig
deeper inside but dreams of poppies, ecstatic red chalices
bowing in a wind she cannot feel.

# THE WOMEN'S WALTZ

—1—

The day overwhelms us with insight into grey. The women survive.
Their chins expand to stubblefields, and the furrows of their eyes
draw closed. In their neglect, these bodies are left to love themselves.

—2—

In fitful sleep inside small cells, time recedes: ethyl-red dripped over
flesh corrodes childhood dreams, drills drone and cigarettes singe grey
skin thinned from years of rape locked in a room. I am here to witness

—3—

the uncanny questions cumbersome bodies pose and answer. Motion
flushes scars; mute mouths like thin knife wounds deliquesce in cold air.
Armed with movement, we are prepared to endure, to perform ourselves:

—Coda—

the women labor to give birth to their body parts before the hour is over.

## REALITY THERAPY

She listens to the hiss of a winged
brown assassin bug caged in the radiator.
Smarting from the effects of reality
therapy and chlorpromazine, Q seeks
solace. Her eyes see that mine fall
into the gaping holes in her body.
I don't say, *You must have a heart,*
*or you wouldn't be alive now*
but recall when I was immured
the punishment of cleaning
with my medieval tongue
cobwebs from the corners
of my stone cell.

She whispers, hand shielding lips,
*My liver is missing.* Lifting
her shirt, she exposes the chasm
where it should have been.
*They took my brain, then my heart.*
*Now I am a tin man. I don't know why*
*I keep letting them harvest my organs.*
*I want to play with ten scorpions,*
she laments. *Those are my friends.*

Stripped of ten of her seventy-eight organs
and flung in the addled face
of neuroleptics, only the scorpion
or cockroach—creatures the sane
want to crush under heel—are good enough
to help. Arthropods guard the jars

lining the morgue, liver and spleen pulsing
pink clouds in turpentine and wine
while dried sticks of lavender
dance from the eviscerated body.

# Dance Therapy

*Let's get your brain back; it is yours,* I say.
I begin to whisper
a series of suggestions: lead
from the cruelly severed space in your head; extend
from the place of most pain.
Winding after your barren brow, flood
the cold cavern of skull with the shock of golden fields, feather
the hawk wings flush against the face, churn
the stream through your mind's crevices, stir
the burgeoning mountains into being.
Next the neck leads, and it arcs and turns
like lilies of the valley in the mouths
of white winds. Cascades tremble
to your shoulders, and elbows lift
with their own breezes. You move
according to your own patterns, the rhythm
of your blood-water, your exhaustive sacrifice, and all
the way down to your feet you reanimate
your life. The dance that warms through you caresses
you into impossible flowers. For the moment you are whole, before
you leave the dance room, before
you die again.

# The Innocent

This asylum is known as *The End of the Road*. At the end
of State Hospital Road, witchgrass overtakes asphalt.
Foxtail cracks cement walls that once enclosed convicts.
Only the window bars remain intact: grim metal mouths.
Headless barbells, rack pulls, and iron boots abandoned
a century ago rust above the silent valley
where hawkswept winds caress muted deer.

Some patients on D Ward have never known this tableau
as they were warned upon entry not to look up: *Never look*
*anyone in the eye if you want to survive in prison.*

The youngest man in my therapy group bares a mouthful of bro-
ken teeth. Saliva seeps through the cracks from heavy haloperidol
cocktails. But when the music rises, he moves with abandon:
from fish-gasping, distressed splashing in air, he kick-turns
full pirouettes, limbs flailing with their own cadence.
With a tenuously controlled fury,
barely missing my face, he reaches up and extracts
from the air something large and wet
that he slaps like a slab of meat
or a missing organ on his shoulders—
then his chest, thighs, waist—slaps transforming to fists,
fists to slicing knives. Somehow, he defies
his habitually hunched stance, head hardly lifted
from chest so he is forced to view the world sidewards,
eyes rolling up as in worship. He defies
his customary gait that suggests skiing on gravel,
tripping to heave himself forward. Instead,
we dance fluently, intersecting rivers.

He crouches and hops off
down the dusty hall like a baby bird,
feet grazing the ground.
He flaps, leaps, and lunges, extending himself boundlessly
to the weak brightness that filters through
the reinforced windows.

Until doctor and techs rush in, inject him with tranquilizers, chastise me
for inciting so much energy. *This dance is dangerous: it encourages*
*sexual urges among men who have raped a paraplegic girl, who have*
*murdered their mothers.* In the ensuing silence the young man meets
my gaze. Innocent children gather in his eyes. He caresses his chest
over the heartache: *There is a tiny animal living here inside me.*

Now that he has found her, he can depend on her—not to haunt
or hunt him, not to flee in fear, but to hold his head upright.
While he dances, he can see, and the bantam, from her perch
protected behind his fervent sternum, is discerning.

## CONVICTED CRIMINAL UNIT—WARD D

*I want to touch art,* A announces. He falls to the floor and wriggles
the iguana out. *How can you touch art?* the others ask. *We can dance,*
he smiles coyly at me. *And she*—his finger thrusts at my head
as he advances, saliva sparkling from his scarlet face—*choreographs
all the dead bodies. Yes,* he turns his accusation and wonder on me:
*You like to slice open the skin and look inside the shoulder. I don't want
you searching in my chest with your knife. I've seen you dissect them
and bring them back to life. You like to choreograph dead bodies.*

The doctors expect me to distract the patients, to exercise leaden bodies
between drug-induced sleeps, but A is right. My real job
as dance therapist is to animate the dead,
to reach inside the chest
like Trismegistus and extract a rousing alphabet,
flood the over-drugged
with fervor.

Be still too long
and you may breed bacteria, flesh-eaters, vitriol rose decomposers.
Be still and you can still
be choreographed; even when the bones degrade,
may you be moved to the stripped soul.

## Discovering the Bones

In motion, every body transforms. We lose our skins and then
our musculatures until pure expression is exposed. M enters the dance
as a conglomeration of pixels. The self-portrait he presents appears
to be a coloring book image of a ripe pumpkin guarded by bleached
skeletons and violet bats. As we dance, he morphs into Krokodil Gena.
*I need a bubble pipe!* Как добраться до костей?

He sweats fragments of Russian with each heavy step. He offers a lesson
in the bones of grammar to the moist and pungent atmosphere. He once
took classes at UC Berkeley until the hospital terminated his time there.
*They aren't satisfied with the term papers I left,* he notes. *Please write
and assure them I'll be back—say I'll donate my bones to Berkeley.*

When I am just bones, shaking and dancing, M says, *You're irrational,
you know that? Why are you just bouncing bones? Let's jump
to the ceiling like leopards.* Then we explore the floor, scattered heaps
of words and skin cells coloring a new context. Searching through
the dust, saffron of Mars and blue litmus, I find it. Just as the light
catches the rough edges, he says, *Hey, give me back my star.*

## THE RAIN

We migrate to the window, two wet hummingbirds trembling the tips of our wings. *Let's look at the rain*, L says, tracing the distant waves with wet fingertip over cold glass.

*Let's rain*, I respond, and we spill from our bodies, soaking our skin, wet seeping from sockets, swaying from sacra, sobs sleeting over noses, spiraling from fingertips. We rain and we rain and we find we are walking in air, stepping across raindrops, through rain and made of rain.

Our feet sprout roots from the soles, flourish fresh green moisture and slick yellow fungus, trees gleaming black in dark afternoon sun. C Ward's grey cracked tiles flush clean. From our roots we nurture trunks and wrap our arms around ourselves, sending nourishment from our feet.

Our skin slips into scrolls, aubades ancient and soft. L nearly fathoms the texture of the primeval material when she remembers: *They drenched me in gasoline again. They're about to strike the flame. Please, give my body to the rain.*

# SCHIZOPHRENIA SPECTRUM UNIT—WARD C

R dances and I translate:

When the wind comes—and it will—the earth will quake, will wiggle
a bit, will move, unrolling a bed, curling a nest. The angels emerge
with tangled hair, dirty hands and feet, and eyes like mine.
Eyes that see as they guide angered waves.

The wolves will memorize the wind in their eyes that causes them
not to see, that stings them with salt so they hurt. They cry and the angels
comfort them in turn by crying back, louder than them; a wailing ensues.
The wail breaks and leaves me at the eldest wolf's knee,
and I pray in her mouth.

I climb into her mouth to pray. She treasures me there, warm saliva
and slight acid of living breath, a cradle flush with wine. Our paws
feel and our snouts scent, in heightened senses; we are warm in this cold.
With hearts too large—with enlarged hearts—we will either die or be in
love. For the instant the dying lasts—or breaks—
we will know both.

## Stomach, God, Glove, and Fruit

R delivers another urgent message:
*The clowns want you to go home-y. Home-y is a place for the clowns.*
*The wolves want you to go home; home is a place that is real; the wolves*
*are in God, and the wolves come from God.*
When we are alone, he confides:
*When we dance with both feet on the ground, we can read the wind*
*we would sense through thick fur were we allowed outside.*
He is another visionary in whom no one stakes faith. Together we are
wolves. We move our paws to feel the breeze and learn from its songs
the ways to move. Sometimes, his words transform to salad
the doctors want to discard as rotten, but the leaves
are nourishing to us. He trusts he can reveal, *I see between*
*the lines between the lines between the lines,*
*and I am telling you.*
I tell him, *I also believe in this between-between; in between*
*is where I become.*
He nods, *Oh, yes, I saw you dancing there.*
We recognize ourselves, and he makes a painting of my movements
he calls *Stomach, God, Glove, and Fruit.*
In the floating stomach glows a fruit. The fruit grows its own tree
from the inside out. God reaches in and twists that tree with a glove.
I too find it painful. I don't want the God-gloved hand to grip
my growing tree and twist it again in His violent fist.
To combat this, we decide upon open palms.
*Open the palm and the eye opens.*
*This is the way of the wolves.*

# The Other World

L is a preschooler who wants to play "London Bridge" and all fall
down on the yellow linoleum where no nurses can see us.
If the doctors notice, they will order their staff to kidnap and trap
her inside the body of an old woman they keep locked in
the psychiatric ward. L treasures memories of nursery school—
swirling finger paints, slipping through Swiss cheese, rolling down
the dandelion hill—before God comes with a man who attacks her
*in the groin*, licks her blood away, drills holes in her hands and dips
his fingers in the waxen wounds. The men take her parents away.
Their bodies gone, *they live in the other world now.*

That is where L wants to go, too. Giraffes roam the other world,
and there are no drills. Just impossibly beautiful creatures
with vulnerably long necks. We dance together until the cages crash
down, her first visit to the zoo so long anticipated. We wiggle our
tails, flex and stretch our claws, sensing the wind on each thick tuft
between calloused yet sensitive pads. We drink the air and listen
with our tongues, howl and flick water from matted fur,
growl, snort, sneeze, then break to blow human noses. L giggles,
enthralled by blue butterflies. One brushes the clockface; the time
to go has passed. As the hour chimes, L collapses with a wail,
clinging to my leg. She begs to leave with me so she will not be
the only furry creature in this hospital corridor, the wrong world
of windowless, concrete cages.

I cannot take her home without being terminated or locked
in a prison cell, but I consider it anyway. I imagine asking Kevin,
*I know you would like a child. Would you adopt a four-year-old girl*
*who appears to be in her fifties and has trouble with fears*
*and sleeping? She likes to be strolled and pushed on the swings.*

Kevin would say yes. I cannot take her and she knows,
yet she is so desperate she heaves herself at the metal doorframe.
As two stoic nurses block her path, L sobs, tremoring her despair,
*Lake, please don't abandon me this way.*

## Acute Unit—Ward B

When the flood comes S grips her chair, copper hair masking
the face marred by gunshot wounds. It was her husband
who pulled the trigger. She sits until something splashes her—
I am not sure what, but I want to find out so I can summon
the notes that revive her. She rises in silence and slithers
to the center. Arms released, hanging heavy, she bows,
lowers her patchwork belly. Twisting the spine, she shudders
with careful purpose, a banded watersnake sensing before
she strikes at what she wants, or needs. Earlier her young
daughters shrieked as she was dragged away; she didn't recognize
them. Sometimes she freezes mid-motion in angular shapes:
toes flexed up, heels crushing down, her slender form stretched
in opposing directions. As she moves, she mesmerizes the voices
that invaded with the bullets, and they fall silent inside her.
When she slumps back in her seat, the rushed voices resume.
Her mouth contorts, arguing something formless.

In her wake, F trembles an invisible bellows between his heart-
pressed palms as though he hopes to inflate his torso. Deflated
at an unnatural angle, he forms a water moccasin's unhinged
jaw, his hands the fangs coordinating all action. He halts
and the room's energy surges through him, contorts him
at odd inclines, then emerges as a soft cough, a hiccup—
no trace of the potential torrents that compelled him to coil.

N prepares for the next flood. He says disaster will strike
in four days. The snakes dancing around him will survive.
Their movement intuitive, their scales resilient, they think
with the body now. N skims the room's perimeter, an old
keelback snake slick against the windows. He has developed

a flickering tongue code to send an SOS. Since the flood nears—
it's just a matter of days now—he carries Styrofoam cups
from his meal tray to the activities room, where he unlocks
tables, books, and catatonic patients in weighted chairs
by washing water over them. Water is the solution
and the devastation. Water is a matter of life. Impending
death is a matter of life now. He does his best to warn us.

# THE CHAPLAIN

The chaplain sighs before his congregation of plastic
chairs, a cartoon yellow Eucharist fixed above the pulpit,
a construction paper halo fading behind his grey head.
Soon the Lord's guests will trail inside, goaded by nurses
and exhausted aides. As the patients have been restless,
it falls to him to deliver the sermon again—to reign in
the unruly spirits, urge them to perform a kindness
for their caretakers, take their meds and exercise patience:
heavenly freedom from mental constraints is a generous
reward. The chaplain no longer notices how the chairs
are affixed to the floor, that the hymn-books are protected
by supple covers. He feeds his audience Christ's passion
in muted tones, God's flesh the antidote to their demons.
One woman raises her hands skyward and an aide subdues
her before she can cry out. Another wants to ask a question
and is quietened. Thus rebuked, the patients stare through
the chaplain as their minds wander away to join the rootless
white clouds. Outside the sealed windows, they rejoice in shifting
shapes, transforming dandelion fluff to dolphins flipping
through feathered sky while the chaplain's voice winds around
their legs like snakes.

## SACRIFICE

H trembles with fervor, fists whitening like strips of fat around bloodless
steaks. She clutches her treasured hands into her chest, bows her crook-
ed neck. She has anointed herself with blood on the forehead: the deep,
cross-shaped crevice tears into her hairline. Her gasps are roadblocks
to her breath; she licks her lips in nervous anticipation, the exhilaration
of exposing something slightly off-limits and secret. She pierces us dead
in the eyes and proclaims: *I want to take Jesus into my heart because I
know only God can fill my emptiness and my special need for attention—*
an insatiable need, a cruel vacuum—*but Satan comes instead.* H slurps
the saliva back between cracked lips. *The Bible says, vengeance will be
God's.* Her grimace exposes a decayed wilderness, the yellowed stumps
of teeth. *But God does not take vengeance. That must be something Satan
says to confuse me.* She refuses her food, spiced with sulfur. *But it's in
the Bible, so I'm unsure. Then Satan grows louder, and I can't hear God
at all.* God is banging both fists on her plastic lunch tray. *I want to do
what they both say, but I can't detect the difference in the voices
anymore. I need them to stop fighting.* To satisfy both—or herself—
she bashes her head against the leaden windowsill and bleeds for them:
God, Satan.

## STOLEN PARTS

When the opening scale of "One Piece at a Time" twangs, waves
of nostalgia rock T to his unsteady feet. Crumbs fall from the old
man's worn green suit, and tears slide down his rutted cheeks.
Soft streams splash the faux wood floor. *Johnny Cash wrote this
song about a man who really did that, built a car out of stolen parts.*
He steps slowly, as though we navigate a world under water, bent
underbelly of light glancing over sunken pasts. *Nothing will be
like that again.* He cringes and loses contact with my hand.
Images of flesh float past in murky depths: he sees himself as a boy
with blonde hair floating on end, then later the series of boys
he devours part by part. The next day, he is ill and writhes in bed;
wisps of dreams pass with puffed white clouds outside steep windows.
Night delivers frost, and the moon comes swollen and red, just as he
remembers. The music tumbles out slightly scratched from a ghost
record, and he is dizzy yet light on his feet, so elated he cannot stop
dancing. Just as he is about to finish reassembling the boys he once
shattered, he wakes up exhausted. The boys dissolve into parts
he cannot reach under the last layers of green sleep.

# THE KING PRINCE

M waits for my dance therapy group to escape his wheelchair.
As the multiple sclerosis progresses, he is doubly confined:
he shakes in his protective straps, staring out between metal slats.
The unit bustles and the staff do not have time. At most, they lift
their lips in passing, call him the football star when he falls, turn
away as he sucks his breakfast from the rubber nipple of a baby's bottle.

When he sees me, M smiles with shark teeth. *Good morning, Queen
Princess*, he heralds; *here I am, King Prince M*. To help him rise
from the grease-slickened chair imbued with the scent of unwashed
years, I hover my forearms over his tarnished throne. With a gentle
pressure on my wrists, he transforms his body's trembling into
a quaking dance—his knees vibrate at the speed of a hummingbird's
wings. After two songs he is steady enough to free one hand
from mine and direct me in a turn. Everybody cheers,
and he never stops grinning. *A true gentleman*, the staff croon.

But today, new patients swarm to us, drawn by percussion
to the room's pulse. M's eyes flare, razing the enclosure
as his unsteady fingers crook and tighten on my wrists. He insists,
*Queen Princess, Baby, My Lover, don't dance with them.
Only dance with me.* The shudder that starts where his claws
enclose me struggles against the surge of promise I felt
moments before when we swayed and his speech traveled
from tripping to lilting, a clear metallic tone
thrown in stark contrast to the rusted iron bars.

# The Mirrors

Grimy slippers shuffle past reflective surfaces, heads ducked
under grey water. Tufts of hair billow beneath, iridescent
in unplumbed darkness. The patients avoid all mirrors.

Today's session is Mirroring. *Let the hips begin. Compose infinite
curves, up and over, around and under*, I say. The weight
of meaning bears us. We exhale, release rather than reach.

Higher is not holier as the priests of dance and culture proclaim.
In the same way the march toward ethereal heights arises
from manipulation, choreography can be a kind of control.

In our dance of reflections, emotions guide the body to movement.
We do not see ourselves cast back but the water that composes us.

My mirror leads from the pelvis, and the anxiety
of enforced stillness transforms her—she re-writes the contours
of bodies and space in incandescent arcs.

C, who always paces the halls alone, stops and bobs his head
in slow motion, engages a greasy table in percussion.
*What you doing in Africa?* he demands.

After squinting into the waves, he shares a look of recognition.
*Oh, you're a black man*, he tells me, *I see. You crossed an ocean.*

The group continues to pulse, a moon jellyfish with many oscillating
ribbons, and Y adds, *When I was born people thought I was white,
too. I didn't get enough grape juice. Here, girl, you better drink this.*

*In this dance, I do not want to know who is leading or following,*
I instruct. *When we move as one in twilit waters, we become reflections.*

For the first time, moist eyes meet mine, trusting that I will follow
any action because bodies transform the moment to meaning.
We navigate our welling contours. They leave their watermarks in me.

My palms beckon, *Come, touch the port of my mouth with blinking*
*hands; displaced across waters and continents, I'll rock with you*
*in our shuddering skiff as you scream.*

# LONG-TERM UNIT—WARD A

L rocks with me as she screams. I cradle her like a broken boat.
The saltwater swells and those on shore keep calling her
by the wrong name. L is a woman who can dance and dream.
N is that child who was tortured with drills and made to bleed.
As grape juice spills down her turtleneck sweater, she screams,
*Stop the bleeding, bring a tourniquet.* She needs one for her head,
legs, arms. I tell myself I can't imagine. (But I can, and I don't dare.)

The outside air is frigid, and she refuses to come in. She does not
want security to *man-handle* her, and she shrinks from the men
who threaten *Murder!* and *Kill!* in the common rooms and beat
on the walls of her cell. One by one, perpetrators are released,
and she stays—twenty years, and she is still shaking, too scared
to come in from the cold. She howls, *My groin is still bleeding
from the drills.*

So I hold our session in the snow where she paces, clutching the iron
bench-swing with hands half frozen. Behind my quilted coat I conceal
my phone so we can watch baby giant pandas play in foreign snow.
In their tumbles and scampers they seem to forget their enclosure.
We decide together to move as the pandas do: the weight
of our monumental, starry heads rocks us forward and back.
We call this *dream-rocking.* On our astral swing, we slice through
frosted winter until we clear a sound path to dream-rock inside.

Rather than patients, dream-rockers are both women and pandas,
so captivating you want to wrap them securely
in your warm embrace, so strong that you cannot dream
of keeping them there.

## The Men's Dance

Some misunderstand. They assume I am here to fold
into their arms, to rock in their embraces, my face tucked
in acrid armpits. They surround me in the smothering space,
concrete closing in, dust particles set to race. Some hurl curses
and gouge each other with jagged yellow nails: *You cunt,*
*she's my woman. No, I am in love with her.* Someone presses
too close and his breath slides into my ear with a promise:
*I'll buy you a space truck, a way out. We'll go to Saturn.*
*I can't wait to lick you. I bet your shit tastes like chocolate.*
He screams, hot saliva spattering my face, then laughs
with delight when he sees I am shaken into parts. I turn in
on myself, try to decipher the writing on the mind's shifting
walls to compose my countenance, but it is cuneiform. Allow me
the pleasure of that mercury. I was a fish. I was never a fish.
More and more I am multiple. I sense the skin splitting,
the blood splintering. I was a hawk, hawk, hawk
and a halfahawk.

# THE DOCTORS

(*Dr. W's laughter spills into the daily meeting room. In the corridor
her voice wears its strong Romanian accent like a cloak, soothing
the women on her ward. She rustles by with a bottle of bright polish
she has brought to paint B's gnarled nails, the yellowed fronds shaking
in her lap.*)

SOCIAL WORKER 2 (*slams the door on* this vulgar scene, *snarling*):
I don't like female doctors. Men make better physicians.
THERAPIST 1 (*joins in the praise of men, extending her criticism
of women beyond these hospital grounds*): This MeToo movement
has gone too far. Now we're expected not to say what we all really think.
(*The DOCTORS nod, their expressions grave, freshly chiseled
headstones. Now that we are on topic,
the THERAPISTS have noticed*): The girls on the unit are asking
for trouble. Only men should be allowed to wear short pants.
DOCTOR 1: Yes, look at S strutting around in those skanky shorts.
Such a whore—I told her, if one of those guys rapes you, you deserve it.
SOCIAL WORKER 1: Good for you. I wanted to say the same thing.
THERAPIST 2: I hope she learns her lesson.
LAKE (*interjects*): I see other patients wearing shorts—
(*Before the dance therapist can say anything more in defense of* that slut,
*the PROFESSIONALS correct her*): Well, the men are not peacocking
around for sex.
SOCIAL WORKER 1: That's right, she just wants one thing
when she wears those trashy shorts.
DOCTOR 2: And she has those nasty, hairy legs. Disgusting.
(*The PROFESSIONALS laugh at the funny double standards.
They know that even if she wanted to shave, her razor is locked away
with her rights.*)

(*B, always in her best, low-cut dress, resumes pacing the hallway,*
*head lowered in shame because the doctors have noticed with the glint*
*of écraseur chains in their eyes her tongue swollen silent*
*and the stubble sprouting on her chin.*)

# The Nurses

The doctor sits behind a closed door guarded by nurses.
The nurses sit behind plexiglass shields that deter blows
and block patients' moans. Those on duty don't look
up as I enter and begin dance therapy.

I sense it must remain secret that I have belonged
on a C Ward. That therefore I have delusions of grandeur
in terms of suffering and *being with* and grant the decay
around me a special kind of beauty, worthy of reverence,
like dance, for its ephemerality. I have looked on this life
as a more authentic incarnation of love. Locked inside,
one strives like a cat enclosed in gloom to soak in
even the smallest shreds of sunlight.

Even though their attention belongs to piles of paperwork,
when the nurses' supposed sole purpose is to keep you,
a stranger, alive with a single-minded fervency that trembles
upon prayer, it occurs to you that this devotion
is the physically enacted definition of love—perhaps
the only one you have known.

## The Asylum's Cats

My dead rest in the time of life before the detoxified substance
emerges from the pillow. Seeps free, exposing the fatal thoughts
that killed them—fine massicot flakes, soft sugar of lead—behind
my sleepless eyes. To represent a sequence of my thoughts,
in order—to demonstrate that they are not disordered—the progressive
is the only possibility for entering into eternal action. Reaction is
all many people have to "fall back on." I do not even want to fall back.
To fall is enough for me. It should be. The unborn are dead dreams,
and I am daydreaming as A and I dance *The Cat Who Desires to Come
in From the Cold and Drink Some Milk Inside Where It Is Warm
and There Are Those Who Love Her (Us, Because We Are That Cat)*.

He sinks to the false-wood floor and drips saliva over his wavering chin
hairs. I am aware that we roll through his spit on the floor. I do not
object to that experience. Experience is what interests us, after all—
progressive tenses, tenses and releases, associations and dissociating.
We love and are loving. A says he dances the cat because he is the cat,
feels sorry for the cat all alone, the cold cat, and *because I drool like a
cat, sometimes on myself.* I do not know any cat who drools on himself,
although I suppose we use our saliva to clean the cruor from our paws.

When we dance, he smiles and his eyes focus, turning toward
the filthy fluorescent lights like a sunflower staring up through black
rain, thick with wet moments, for the source of dazzling life. He wears
the same unnaturally green sweatshirt as yesterday and the day before,
a crumb from morning snack shining on the shoulder. His eyes become
bluer, or perhaps just deeper, the longer he smiles. When winter comes,
he demands the doctors admit the feral cats waiting outside
the window for remnants of warmth. When the doctors dismiss him
with placating palms on his shoulders, he hisses, sinking his teeth
into their milk-soft hands.

# THE ASYLUM'S DEAD

Alone in my office: rough stone becomes dust; orb weaver spins silver
shadows in the frost; those who died in bondage beneath slowly begin
to trace the contours of my feet. A blizzard drives the other therapists
away, warm at home, and the dead begin to sift to the surface. They
have heard the patterns of my feet and the arcs of my leaps. They see
me struggle to follow the head's lead, rivaling the panic that keeps me
frantic in all directions—window—window—door—out past the trees.

And under the snow, frost knives light the last grass blades; beneath
frozen soil rustle the old bones against which all new patients weigh
the same dashed wishes. The dead begin to play with me—or have they
come to pray? Like a dance of contact improv, gauzy fingerbones stroke
the decline of my shin to the ankle and direct my strength to the dirt.
Smooth my scapula, stitch the shoulders, and expose my chest embers
skyward. You, the disembodied, tap my clavicles and release quivering
laughter from a crooked bow, swing toward my elbow, swift spiral
away. Make me pivot, disoriented—but in the direction of trust.
Stretch back the cervical spine and laugh as I join you
on the mossy tombs. Let the snow seep into my blood and show me
what you know I should know. How is it to be you confined first
to this prison hospital and now to the earth holding your forsaken
hospital cell?

This time when I rise, mud and slush drip from my hair and eyes. How
was it you wanted to say? —not *what* was it, for if you could talk
in the way society demanded, you may have died elsewhere, perhaps
at home in a bed. *How* was it, and I will dance it for you. I know
what it is to be misunderstood.

## The Tunnels

Shackles hang slack
in the subterranean damp
where the noncompliant
patients once were kept.

Iron bands caressed raw wrists,
the faceless woman stripped
of life, children, shoestrings when
the husband desired a younger mistress.

Prisoners tried for atrocities
and found guilty of insanity
strained into their irons, the executions
underneath, their resurrections incomplete.

Winter days when corridors crowded
with the poor huddled for heat,
the mad were culled and sent beneath
to limit hangings, not lobotomies.

Above the arctic tunnels the townsfolk
remained in the dark. Irreverent feet
passed over the asylum's sunken heart
where the florid blood of buried lives still seeps.

These grounds are not haunted by ghosts
long forgotten but by men in white coats
who approach the stone altar with diplomas
that disintegrate in dulcifying flames,

no fire-cured experience
of ecstatic visions, no unknowing cloud
of hallowed psychosis.

# A Dance of Death

Where prayer and war crime coincide
the doctor performs a trepanning on the past.
My autumn is doveless and grey prematurely.
Outside, the female animals live closer to God.
The doctor is drilling a hole in the skull
to flush the demons from the poor
possessed.

A psychiatric assault: neuroleptics
spawn cumulus clouds over minds fraught
with memories. I, the dance healer, bow
over the dying to inhale the last breath,
save the spirit in my lungs, then don
the corpse's last clothing, threadbare
from anonymous washings: the archimine
in green hospital gown.

# RESTRAINT

Opaque rooms fall in line behind four pairs of metal doors
and twice the number of locks and keys. From the stale gray
cloud appears the imposing iron chair with weighted leather
straps for head, neck, wrists, waist, ankles, and two solitary feet.

The ground is graced with scuffs from shoes, laces removed,
scarlet nail polish scabs left by strangled bare toes thrashing
after the grass they will never again feel, no trace of the feet
swaddled in sticky-soled socks all hospitals issue except
the rancid scent of fear steeped in breathless acrylic sweat.

The silence is a grey smoke; the camera obscures your face.
In the room with padded, grey walls, any restraint is for your
safety. Still it seems that punishment is devoid of movement,
is, in fact, the lack thereof—the promise of perpetual stillness.

# FLORID

*Echolalia* is a lovely word.

Religion is the language we have to express our fears. Or,
religion is the culmination of human fears packaged as narrative.

*Floridly psychotic* is a beautiful image for a frightening time.
Blood and red become flowers indiscriminately upon leaving
the body, bursting through the yellowed air behind closed rooms.

Last night I woke with splatters of blood like soft mist or fine paint
over my skin and underclothes. It was simply—and astonishingly—
the poppies beginning to grow, to erupt from me, with great effort

from my organs: my heart, strangling pain into love. Blood to poppies,
in poppies, sleep to life. So is *histrionic*, so is *dysphoric*. Vermillion,
a cinnabar sentence.

I understand. I too will be hospitalized soon.

# Now I Am Immured

P appears with bleeding lips, pleads with me in a pressured voice for
cocaine, a lawyer, to kill someone. The patients address me as *Satan*
and *Snake* because I move my hips and urge them to dance
every detail. They are my people. No amount of alprazolam
or heaping pile of prazosin, no variety of tricyclic can ease them through
shrieking nights and pacing days confined to gray halls, gray cells
with green plastic masking gray beds, where everything is made
too heavy to be hoisted and thrown. Nothing should break
but the patients—into blooms of psychosis, flowers of phosphorous.

My people fall to the floor when they dance and edulcate to great
pandas, greater than themselves and strong as they are gentle, stroking
the bamboo floorboards and their soft bodies, alternately six and sixty
years old. I no longer know whether L exists or whether she is a part
of me I simply misremember as a separate person, a patient locked in
a lightless state ward whom no one will live to tell about "outside."

In our dance sessions, we become fiercer animals together. She sees me
as a red panda when I walk past her cage, reminds me to *stop*
*and nourish yourself at the great tree outside.* I am many, and some of us
cannot breathe under the wet woolen blanket of anguish and despair,
where those who are vindictive piss in the radiators and kick
the therapists and those who are hopeful hide from the needles
or press themselves against the smudged windowpanes watching
for prisms of light—triangles of euchlorine, toxic and bright green—
to pass over them, to pass through on their way somewhere else, flowers
of antimony in white flux. Ghost-blue faces wave, breathless
with fulminating silver, explosive if they touch the air outside.

I did not have a chance to say goodbye.

# III:
# THREE KINDS
# OF MADNESS

## UNEMPLOYED

*for Sister Barb*

Open the swan cell and free their feelings. Look beyond this squalor.
They do not belong behind frostbitten ribs, nor to this perpetual winter.
Sister says, *This is your passion now.* She is the architect
of the primordial feeling, the unemployed angel. Slowly, she loses
breath, sinking through one of many soft, yet painful, clouds.

## Cirrus Scar

There is a mare's tail between a wound.
A scream cuts a cloud in jagged halves.

## THE NEW ANGEL

It is as though you are being prepared for sacrifice. Lost
on unnamed trails, you decide to disseminate yourself. The solution
is not watered-down. It is water. It turns out, you are being erased.

The men try to infect you with their evil, but you are medieval
in your mysticism as in your diseases. Smelling too much basil
may breed a scorpion in the psyche. To cure ague, swallow
the web of a silver spider wrapped in the remains of a raisin.

The pharmacists synthesize a tablet from the sulfuric breaths
of spirits dyed a caustic chemical white, the cast the color
of forgiveness, the substance that of silence. Unlike the outspoken
ancient heralds, they call it the new angel. *Cum fossa et furca*
they whisper into the drowning pit, the silent capital punishment.

Seek asylum in a field specified only in the maps of your dreams.
You have never been lost even if no one outside has succeeded
in mapping the terrain. Don't let them fell the trees and burn
the pages. If you must ingest something soundless, let the pills
be previously unheard prepositions and articles. Love the indefinite best.

# THE WOLF

The wolf is chasing me. I cannot let her near, but I must keep her
where I can see her soft fur. She is here to kill me. I knew she would
come. No one else understands she will kill me. They ply her with cash
and ask her politely to leave. In her human form, she tucks the money
in her pocket and pretends she will not approach. Then they turn
their backs, saying, *See? All okay.* As she advances, she looks straight
at me, sharp wolf's eyes penetrating blue, and confides, *It's hardest
on us.* And resumes her pursuit, tries to enclose me in padded rooms,
but I escape.

For days I sensed she was on the way, and when she first arrived
from far off, she was smaller and blue and not yet a wolf. I screamed
and no one came. Now she grows larger from chasing. Now she is
a wolf. Is she one of me? I will not eat myself, will we? And what if I do
not want to become her and die? Because I know, in this convoluted
vision of vitality into which I rose, only the hunted can survive
with voice. The hunted alone—the severely alone—have the choices.
Though my wolf may love, only my prey may be selfless—and in
that moment of weakness when the wolf knows she loves the wolf,
she loses her life.

## I Wake in the Asylum's Phosphorescent Night

Sometimes the day, the earth, the tremble, the other, the anti-
and the antidote are all of you. I woke with no feeling in my arm,
but the phantom limb held flowers. My reach is also hindered

by my backward hands. I'd love to stay, and I prefer to go inside
the cabinet where, even with the expansive striped cat, there is room
to be hidden. I feel ready and I feel better and better. Decadence

is a way for uneasy eyes, and owls come by courageous lineage,
uneasy over the emptiness. The cabinet is not a proper nest;
things may disappear outside. I try carrying a message: the urgent

mouse in my mouth shivers the significance for those who participate
in the body's language. My phantom limb begins to flood flowers
where there might have been blood, were I human again.

## Night Ablution

My unborn children dangle from my beak
between shining enamel bars of teeth.
I brush and brush but my ideas for human life
just gestate to death. I swallow miasmas
of my venom and their first choking breaths.
Only their tails still swing, foaming
from my lips sweet heart rats or grass snakes.
The unborn digest me, powers flicker weakly.

My fingerprints have worn off completely.
Will we revive the avialan I am and might
have been? The doctors are prejudiced against
the unfound source—they think, therefore,
unfounded—in this unknown creature.
They drink me a bit to test my likeness.

## The Doctor Orders

A man in white slurs his voice, tongues the letters
as though he cannot discern the different shapes
of words. He wants to appear romantic

by dressing himself in silks from sweatshops
milking the Bombyx mori and their white leaves.
He seeks to sound as though he reigns from a cloud,

pitching his weak voice from the mulberry tree.
Toss the children candy and stooped men
scoop it into billowing grocery bags, hoard

the shining foils in a drawer until they bleed syrup.
Toss the patients plastic prizes they are obliged
to touch to their lips, bitter pellets of praise.

Forced to drink from the cup they must kiss,
only then may we be released.

# Emet

The narrowing stairs continue to climb.
Files, papers litter the wells.

Everyone who has claimed and gained
the authority to destroy me is present
behind the yellow eyeglasses.

When I created this intricacy, I fashioned
neither peak nor locked tower, though
requested by my patrons, my killers.

Now they want to know what lies beyond
the labyrinthine ghetto.

There is no end if they kill me. I am
the associative key, and the doctor
holds the golem to the letter.

## Erasing the Aleph

The social contract specifies sitting, perpetually immobile
in this context—in agreement with the man who ties me
in strings, thin as dental floss, but pastel in colors to make
the pain resemble more the setting rainbow, reassembled
from the colors of my body. But as thin strings slice
the tender skin, the rainbow pools on the parquet. All men
are our fathers. All our fathers tell us lies when it comes
to their pleasures; it is untrue that men dislike pink.

## -KINESIA

I cannot relax
because the white-gloved men
will kill me.
Even without hands, I am tactile,
like the child tucked inside
the dark.

## INVISIBLE MURDER

The man tried again to kill me by weaving a fishing wire
through sixty thousand miles of veins as I slept. I woke
in the net, but the net was inside me. No one else could see
the knots he had left.

## Visible Murder

Denying my body a place to grieve, the musician extends
my ligaments into a stringed instrument like the medieval
Katzenklavier. He caresses the keys fashioned from molars
that tauten my tendons, releasing the mallets' steel claws,
the creature's melodious cry. The needles enter like eyes.

# BLOODLINES

Someone called me by the wrong name and my other appeared.
Writing is nondifferent from sleeping on land. I departed
on a quest to find a field specified only in the maps of my dreams,
hypergraphs cast by spiraling stars strewn across cold water.
My function is to locate a feeling beneath.

(!╬ ↕⋮⸴⋮· Dig the nails in to sense the flesh. ⸮⸮⁀⸮⸮ ꞊ · ≡)

The iceberg on the socio path was the one to preserve the man.
He clenched a spear in his teeth and a penis in his hands
and was frozen at the climax. Predators mistakenly seek the white
drifts at the tip, unaware of the depths of blue. Hunters have faith
in the ordinance of their victory.

(↙∞↗ Pelts gnashed between the teeth, pubic hair hangs on his lip. ♂⋮'⋮↓)

Even in the failure to become fluid, he believes the light from many
futures lilts over his ice embedded territory and someone will stumble
upon the true human in his race.

))))>    <((((  <((((  <((((

## WHITE NOISE

You lost your last apostle when you anesthetized me.
There is no good way out of sleep. We believe the hawk
holds more mercy in one talon than does the man in his white
coat who says, *Portray your end of the ghost with the shadow
departed.* That is how you know you have survived—
the shadow leaves you. And though you may dig endlessly
through the body parts of the dead for your phantom limb,
that is not your way. Speak to the foliage bowed to the other
broken birds, their beaks sutured shut in the underbrush.

## CIRCLING

The hawks watch and know. Circles are successful.

## Encircled

Lonely, my stars elongate the passageway of my throat that leads one
galaxy into the next. I am pregnant there by the stars' schizo affect.
Their iron brightness perplexes some, but they illuminate a scarf
I must knot when the stars feel stimulated, rocking
silver skiffs on my gilt brainwaves, dangling
me hanged by the warm neck.
I always resurrect.

## BEDLAMITE,

Take one life
to make a poem
you can live in.
Take all your lives
to make this home.

## Burnt Yarrow

All water is good water. No water
can be bad at being water.

When dispatched to the world,
the participants' particles congregate
in new constellations; they are now
more they than they ever have been.

My emissary is blue. That particulate,
arrived from the middle ages, augments
in my iris, complements the medieval
ascetic in my mind, severed hands
praying under the pillow.

My cavern for the spoken wind
brims with leaves becoming brittle
as my incarnations grow more malleable.
The suggestion is to find the white plague,
go inside, and grow. We will emerge
a cloud of orange smoke.

## SAVIOR HAWK

It is a shame to die in the sand,
a mistake to fall in the freezing rain.
One tail is softer than weather.

I love her—the blackness beneath
a bright blossom. Umbrellas bloom
around my relief, prone in the street.

There is one who sweeps effluvium,
unfolds the rope I curled, burns the tubercle
cottage to make my bed of down and rain.

My savior, hawk, watches me
from her wire.

## Buttercups in a Bag Around the Neck

Bells around the ankles of the treasured bird track her motion
or help her glisten. A man clutches at her throat. Long ago
her daytime broke. The unknowing cloud around her beak

shrouds the wisdom she moves in vast monuments, expanding
a space more violet, a nest of lilacs for those who must step
through blazing sand. Caress the clavicles, the bag of buttercups

strung around the neck. Inside the hollows of the bones about
to crack hide other refugees—medieval girls struggling to prolong
their dancing sickness. They abhor the fate of grown women—

murder for their sex, necks snapped in the hands of bearded men.

## THREE KINDS OF MADNESS

Talk fast to yourself in your sleep. Now is the time for mysterious
apparitions. Weave under the time and over the time the pink heads
of roses. Ex out the courageous wooden figures with your axe:
the carpenter, the cross. Ancestral deities loosen the ropes around
your-my wrists and plunge stones into the pond, finished starting
fires in our mouths that are nothing more than smoke signs, methyl

orange. The wind leavens and leaves red. The ideas you trust most
might have been your progeny, but they emerged in pieces
from your wounds. They continue to exit now as apparitions—
from the holes in your feet some eyes, from the gash in your side
a cracked and fingerless hand, from your wrists the mingled blood,
and from your head another head crowns. From the birth canal pulse

several hearts—three—darkening the outside air and darkening
the passage, and through your labia the apparition of some thorns
blocks the exit and entrance. No one comes or goes this way.
To wish you strength, you are given a bouquet by those who keep you
in the hospital bed, alive and warm. You fear the flowers will fall
through your quaking palms, but the bouquet is a circle of thorns.

# Host

Just a taste and the body's guests want you for a savior.
Soft road of mud, treacherous light bearing bridge.
Even if you jump, the alters will lift you up;
each has staked a claim within. The reliquary casts
its net of burning light upon the naked altar.

There are profits in madness so long as we are kept
in chains. The ward's first distinguished guests arrive
with wafers and wine. They toast their providence as they watch
the madwomen rave, rattle hair mattresses, scratch
black, oozing scabs the mad-doctor has made.

Mercury numbs blue gums, cages slip into silver-puddled
silence, cold muscles slap concrete. We never tire
of speaking for the insane, in tongues, of flicking the worm-
ridden and despoiled meat. Pink skin peals away from the brows
and the next face is still ours. It's not that we are brave;
the host has lived already through the times of plague.

## Trinity in Spectral Coordinates of Green

The same vast green window keeps passing
overhead, projecting the same view—a triangle,
the top of a house crooked by misshapen moon,
sickle-celled branches of moonlight breaking off
and dropping white dust within a dead house,
the place rustling with tarpaulins to catch the chalky
fallen skies, the decomposition of the cell.

The abbess is left in center, illuminated like pages
of the manuscript. Beautifully bright letters swerve
over her skin. Meanwhile, the window overhead
shifts slightly, a tremor, an illness, or hallucination
being born in the quarters where she is kept. Meant
to proffer a semblance of moon or sky, the window
puts her under. The angle erases one of her eyes.
The corner frame falls across her mouth, misshaping.

Exposed to the green triangular light, the dead baby
roosts on the golden throne, the soft bouquet
of poison parsley barely brushing blue lips.

## PROTECTOR

It is too late to say whether Saturn holds a cure.
The dead baby rocks in her green basket beyond reach.

The silver day is gentle as the angel's hair is long.
Flowering like a wedding gown in a strong

headwind, she stumbles over schorl locks
and long strands entangle her or tear out,

bleeding from the scalp, but she never falls.

Intoxicated by her sorrow, the million blue butterflies
rush back between her lips. A humiliating hope lords

it over us, ignores her blue origins. Watchmen stumble
over the yellow in the night. She is no angel

of mercy, this bourgeoise possession performed by the loneliest,
rung-climbing ghost who curls up next to us.

We lie half-dead in white dust, dreams exposed.
From the gouged stomach emerge the red flower bones;

the wind left softens the death
of poppy and recollection.

## CARBO ANIMALIS

The bread of sadness:
it is the bread made
with ashes. I compose
a dance for ten gallons
of hair that hold ten
hundred heads'
different memories.
Outside, the train
shrieks its terror.

## ANIMA

The archangel appeared and commanded: *Woman,
lower animal, Man will grant you the gift of his sex.*

You are God's lover. You have but to raise the animal
to your lips. The chalice overflows with uteroplacental
gifts.

# CAPITULA

The voice makes me shudder; rain shudders the doors to the cold
down my spine that open outward like the gleaming leaves left
on the flower bone. Do not desire my parts; my mind never parts
with the body kneeling in tenebrae. Do not stab your silver knife

into my neck. Work it around, twirling, twisting. Say, *don't take up
space, woman.* I am a woman, and I love space. Do not show
your eyes woman. Latitudinal directions you contemplate complain
to overseas brothers who beat you in the end while it is ending.

Careful what wood you touch when you enter the flowers' house.
You may bask in the unmuted light of knives there; for the first time,
flowers gleam scalpels through their golden eyes. When the blade
encounters immutable iris and transmutes silver, it reflects the face.

The eye of the solar flower looks on. The radius extends up-
and outward a black wheel like a spider strangling her glittered web.
Cotton mother. Spider squeezes the body to keep her calm, unyielding
innocent creature. Strangle star dangles from her vulva on mucus

that is beautiful, that is courteous, that eliminates non-colors
from the energies winding the world. Strepitus also extinguished.

## SPECTRUM

There is no measure. The table is wrong. The grammar
has been sewn on. When walking on water, be careful
of the consumptive lungs, the waterlog. Safe, incorrect
presence. I see the feet under the door. The shadows
are wrong. Because I am starving, people are concerned
about whether I know God. Worrisome not to remember
myself. Too cold behind the green prism. Am I
on your golden snake list? The snakes are ready
for therapy. Ten a.m. and boundaries are permeable.
The time to touch the air in between arrives. God locks
the ceiling overhead, the box closed too much. Stumbling,
my disabused balance is the texture of a moth's wing.
A whole desert appears from the powder of the dark blue
eyespots. Darkened day flutters before exile to brown.
They say, *I'll place forks in you.* How many are there?
Metal tines in flesh.

## BENEDICTION

How many serpents does your heart hold?
God's creatures need a space to live that is
both soft and hard enough. Counting backwards
from the end of numbers, the rain sloughs off
the skin: you are shedding your first corpse.

The drug is assembling a bomb in the stomach compiled
of all the dregs of dread, like a fish reassembled after
she is hooked, slaughtered, slit, eaten, and digested.
But the dismembered mouth still gasps
to kiss the feet of the Bird of Love.

I squat and play with my children, revenants,
on the frozen sand floor. On the shores of the Lake,
I carry my own little ghost curled in my arctic palms.

I am too cold in my dreams. Despite the icy air, a cuprous
statue of my hand unfolds green, prepared to cultivate
emerging flesh wounds. Spring will come and with it new
ghosts, freshly sprouted from the hearts of the snake.

And always I am drawn to the traces of the loved one's
shining talons. Her imprints fall to pieces in the snow
where I lift them to blue lips. I fall to my knees
and dash my kiss on ice; it crumbles
and dissolves beside delight.

## PATIENT

Today the doctor is expecting a spectacle,
a death parade for all wide-eyed onlookers,
the march on the asylum to effect a less
fluorescent light. Under his scrutinizing gaze

we stoop in a line with ragged edges. The clock
hangs bruised on the battered wall of flesh. Techs
perform a body search and the muted patients
stand down, empty hands outstretched.

But a white-haired woman clutches her doll
with lips that reveal faint incisors of life,
and every sixteen seconds the plastic mouth spills
miraculous baubles in time with our delirium tremens.

## PRAYER OF AVIAN INTERCESSION

On the floor where everything is murder, among sutured beaks,
he lifts a fine bone to his nose. Without recognizing the origin,
he knows he has bathed in the blood. Somehow, he disremembers
his return here, to his place of salvation. Curled beneath the piano
bench, hoping the keys would shoot sounds through his skull
to help him find his face, he was masturbating to the murder—
he remembers now—when he requested to be saved. Ask Sister
Barb to light another candle, perch it on the dream tree so it flickers
and inflames the hermitage where she lived a life for every penitent
who lies among the bones he has broken, not knowing to whom
to return the femur, the pinion with quill and barbs still suspended.

## The Penitent is Branded by Three

Someone will *see* me to death,
and I experience guilt for all of it—
I suffer medieval mysticism

that my murderer attempts
to extinguish.
This is our symbiosis:

a body made of threes,
the ashen triangle too shining.
This is why I panic

when I no longer can read the star signs
etched in green on my body of trees:
the carvings cleaved by humans

clutch deep inside,
and the hypergraphic scribes
relinquish nothing.

# SCIVIAS

Afraid of losing my irrevocable words, I root for them in the dirt,
shredding loaves of green bread with my nails to find the heart,
shuddering the mass of leaves in procession. I beg the doctor
to prescribe me a new preposition, as though he has any power
over the meanings among words. After my burial, you will find
my intention lost at Lake's edge. A sharpened blue star—sharper
than anything conceived by human materials—slices though my skull,
the coffin, frozen earth—and rises like a fatal flower. Who knows
with what harm or joy it will bless the next animal who scents it out
and loves it before swallowing its counterintuitive edges. Beauty is
contraindicated for survival, though not for our conception.

# ORDER

Uncollected memories spin in any order, flooding back
such that with my childhood come sex crimes,
and only later I learn to brush my teeth, then open my eyes.
Someday I see a hand with two fingers drawn,
the crucifix prepared for me in an empty schoolyard.

The children in plaid uniforms applaud the head upon the platter.
In their obedience they learn to love the feast. At the head
of the table their petite wooden savior rests his cheek
upon his shoulder. He will never finish sacrificing himself
to himself. And beside his heart my ravening wolf first speaks.

Shrike impales her soft prey—a smaller bird's small belly—
on the thorns she cultivates in her shire. Her happiness, like
her horror, emanates a shriek in Old English. What comes after
the last intestine? The children cheer when the butcherbird,
ghost of the dead son, descends to strike their tongues on fire.

*Your problems are caused by storing too many worries between*
*the ear and the jaws. Your mind is unusual, your body too small.*
Stricken with organic stigmata, paroxysmal spasms, I speak
a hereditary silence, incant wind and worm, swan and tower.
In place of darkness, unbroken pallor. I ended every story

with ascension. A blood-red cardinal lifts a ballooning aorta;
the pupils inflate soft beach balls behind the priests' robes,
but nothing rises more than a few feet; the drawn Catholic girls
exposed in plaid skirts hover weakly, legs dangling. And all
day long, the cadavers of dead animals are washed onto shore.

## DRAGGING THE LAKE

We dredge to see the outlines of dreams
surface and sink—iterations of another
life—the great broken possessions of the dead
and the ways we deprive them by keeping them
ghosts. The color gray is all they have to eat.
We do not let them climb from the Lake's silken
cold. We never expected their dreams to float.
We are cruel when we believe we are living.

# The Night Comes

It is time to choose who survives.

# Kind Darkness

We do not have enough words for darkness, the mutations. In time
the kinds will equal the ocean. We can no longer endure the confines
of an embrace. A chalice shines darkly with my venomous blood.
My keepers comb the garden for the poisons I wept, clutching
my revenants to my chest. They bind the body to coax the demons out.

All are sad for they who devolve within the womb, smothered
by the right hand. We perform our divinations by means of a ritual
laughter, sew leaden vespers into the white coat pockets of our confessor
before he approaches the river to drown our madness in stones.
Otherwise, he would claim and baptize the earth. Christ is the Verb

who delivers the danger. In a devastated sky the sun is hanged, black
sackcloth of coarse hair. Horses pass afloat outside. In tenebrous garden
waves the sea where we will be cast, the dreamstone knotted around my-
our neck. Imagine, the audience—hungry doctors in alabaster jackets—
are appalled when it does not weigh us down as contrived. In kind

darknesses we lack the language to sleep. The currency of hope is still
light. The soul issues a contrafugue, and we weep into our nests by night.
Dreams drip from our bloody stitches. The phlebotomist whets his fleam,
but it is unsafe to leave. Christ appears by vision and slips the holy
foreskin in the medieval mystic's open mouth, asks us to treasure

the host. Our confessor envies the croques-prépuces who lick their lips
when they finish testing whether the foreskin is genuine so as not to risk
crumbs lost to cloth, flesh wasted upon napkins. They cry under cover
of darkness staring at Saturn's rings. We lie down without words
in our mouth, but how can we rest? There is a body between God and us.

## Witch Pricking

The doctors keep pricking me to be certain I am not a threat.
Until now, each time the phlebotomist approaches with needles,
I have bled profusely and been allowed to live. But because
too many lives have extinguished in me and returned to earth
unborn, new nurses arrive and scratch lines from one mark
to the next, charting freckles, sunspots, scars across
my goose-fleshed pelvis and chest. They search for a site
with secret meaning, a pock that when pricked will stay arid,
proving once and for all that I am a witch. My own powers
of tenacity will exile me to the mist-yawning hole beneath
the street where the other psychotic, now homeless, prophets
curl in restless sleep. The mad-doctors who have inscribed
their names on the white bands around my wrists prick to ascertain
whether I am possessed by anyone else. On that inevitable day
when I open my mouth and no more blood trickles out,
only these clean words will spill, condemning us.

## DEAD CART

The corroding cart flakes purple rusted
skin, buboes burst into shapes of soft hearts
you may peer through, but no trace remains
of the bodies that bowed to the plague,

their names ground under articulate wheels
many years ago now. The half-life
of the black death is thirty days. The half-
life of my fear is thirty generations.

## Know the Ways

The angels have flocked south for winter. The last
old man saw them go—even angels do not pass alone.

## HAWK REPRISE

Sunrise falters, repeating flickers. Smooth surface catches fire, owls
leap from branches, the vole creates a cavern so deep he may never
emerge. The space seems to collapse upon us and shudders the legs.

The grotto closes and fish smile for the first time. I loosen my suit
and venture one bone out. Air quickly devours it. My hawk continues
to watch over us, repeating herself every few meters. She is perfect

though exposed to freezing memories, though she stands alone
in the open minds. The medical staff who keep me huddle behind
a wall and whisper. Their "sss" and "shhh" sounds carry—

clicks and snake speech reverberate overhead. Who can carry out
corrections, grammatical or physical, from behind a wall? A wall
is not an adequate disguise. I can see through it. I tell them,

*You are not the hawk; therefore, you have no feathers, no authority.*

## WAKE THE WOLF

It is time to reenact your morning.
The pilgrimage is underway.
Rocks sharpen beneath your feet.
Fireflowers shiver to straw,
bursting brown stones into autumn.

Holes dapple the air, tiny black
specks as in lungs or yellowed
photographs. You age. All at once,
the life you refused catches you,
welling a wave half fire, half fur.

You are made from coywolves hunting
madly for the den, reading the moss
on slick roads, decaying the winter
into a wet cold, life dripping
from your white teeth.

## PILGRIMAGE

Tired humans pass, bent forward,
easing into their pain, grey umbrella
bent at the seams and bewildered.

The dead mumble together with earth
in their mouths. Passersby do not understand
their sayings; they are making plans for the long
day after. There is a new minister of loneliness.

Do not berate the dream conceived
in the asylums: no sound, just volume.

Of every crime for which I am tried
in my sleep, I wake guilty.

The dream becomes corrupt,
incredible as his vision
and the monolith who survives as man.

Corrugated times granted the nomadic
intelligence, but the change to change
proves too much by mid-way.

In the religion of water, there is no evil;
darkness is a mystery that uncoils always.
My inheritance is a woman made of souls.

My body still holds the smell
of the creature who wore it before this.

## THE HUNTER DESIRES THE CREATURE

I woke up still alive,
but there he was, kneeling
by my bed with a knife, trying
to devour my ghost.

## THE NEW SKY

We thirst and the horses offer
us to drink from the pouring
wounds of night before the seagull
slides over, towing the new shades,
swinging us irrevocably under.

## MALIGNANCY

We are made to drift on thoughts
golden as birdflocks that darken
unswerving shadows over Lake.
Obscure black nodes hover opaque
as clouds of flies but packed
with the men who want to kill us—
like a cancer of sky and water
where only blue is susceptible:
a cerulean-eating sepsis.

## PROGNOSIS

The body landscape has been colonized—
by whom and what, and for how long now?

Who is left to read the landmarks of historical
significance: stretches of worship and ritual incision,

pilgrimage trails eclipsing unfathomable caverns,
healing other worlds at the hands of my eyes.

Incurable sky. Beyond grey-green gates,
this sky is the other sky's refuse, our white

the other light's opaque plague. Pain is eminent—
like ecstasy welling the blood—the source

of a congregation of greater contagions: dance
until our guests collapse. Gentle purple bleeds

from the poppy left to die upon the floor.

## PROPAGATION

My mind is the poppy field,
      exquisite blood-reds waving
in the wind of ghost voices
      the doctors harvest for opium
to inject the dead when I fall
      to sleep. I cannot afford to lose
my flowers' silken whispers.

Whom will they inject,
      feed on my visions?
            Who will be me next?

## WALKING AGAIN OUTSIDE THE ASYLUM

The length of iced-over desert stretches absent arms.
Ghost traces clot the horizon, frosted moisture corroding
the restraining chair left to rot. A hawk bursts from the jagged
seat, flushes our faces with warmth, the glow of knowledge
and danger. The watchman attempts to warm his unfeeling
fingertips in the weak light of the patients' flickering prayers.
The people are disturbed, both inside the gates and out.
Our prayer is cold like God's articulate fingertips, like
his delicate wrists; we are sick. The hawk repeats her passion.

## The Trial

Be careful to cover your tracks. You have revealed
too much, especially what moves in between Lake
and sky. Pull back the door that animates the ghosts
of colors, tossed to celestial graves. The way between
is annealing. The sky will be sealed now.

# Glossary

>)))): basic unit of symbols employed in this collection to transcribe crow speech; the character shapes and their augmentation evoke sonogram depictions of crow language.

Как добраться до костей: How to get to the bones. The patient quoted often spoke phrases in Russian.

**Alchemy**: medieval chemical philosophy and science meant to transmute so-called base metals to pure gold, generally sanctify or sweeten, and create cures. In this collection, the alchemical terms are especially significant for their magically-extracted or intuitively-incanted colors.

**Aleph**: first letter of the Hebrew alphabet and first letter inscribed on the brow along with mem and tav to make the golem self-animate. To destroy a golem brought to life by inscribing one of God's names on his clay head, the aleph is erased, leaving only mem and tav, or met, which means death.

**Alprazolam**: oral chemical compound given as a fast-acting tranquilizer; one of the benzodiazepines of the triazolobenzodiazepine class. Also causes memory problems, depression, fatigue, risk of suicide, and a two-fold risk of mortality by any other cause.

**Angel**: unborn ghost who wishes to wear human flesh.

**Anima**: Latin term that predates soul. Referred to the "rational soul" and "mental intelligence" considered properties of masculine humans made in God's image and historically used to discount and prove inferior factors like multiplicity, emotion, and physical knowledge designated as feminine.

**Archimine**: ancient or medieval medical-spiritual professional employed to breathe in a dying person's last exhalation and thereby save his or her essence.

**Associative key**: Lake Angela, or translator for associative, schizophrenia spectrum expression into neurotypical human verbal language as ordered by the rule of logic.

**Asylum for the Insane**: original name for many psychiatric institutions, including Osawatomie State Hospital, founded 1866, and from which Part II: Asylums derives.

**Aubade**: in medieval times, a morning love song or poem of lovers greeting the dawn.

**Benediction**: invocation of divine aid or blessing; also refers to the Catholic practice of exposing the host, or a piece of the transubstantiated body of Christ, to the gathered Mass for their worship. Usually caged within a golden monstrance, the body part should bless the devout by its presence.

**Blue litmus**: blue pigment extracted from lichens that transforms to red in the presence of acids and back to blue if bases are added.

**Blue otter**: North American mammal thought to produce poison secretions.

**Bombyx mori**: the domestic silk moths who eat white mulberry leaves and osage orange and are now dependent upon humans for reproduction, after which the humans steal their silk.

**Butcherbird**: Old English name for the shrike.

**Buttercups**: the golden flowers worn in a bag around the neck during times of black death to act as a cure for insanity.

**Cacogenic**: in eugenics, those "poorly born" believed to bear a genetic flaw in the germ-plasm; the opposite of the so-called eugenic. The degenerative or undesirable elements who spread mental illness with their "bad seed" are still deemed unfit despite the outdated terms.

**Capitula**: the head of a flower, including its florets; in Latin, a chapter, an index preceding a Gospel, a typographic symbol, or a brief reading from the Liturgy of the Hours; gnathosoma of ticks or mites; a genus of barnacles; part of the mimicry of ants by other organisms; part of the female Lepidoptera (order of insects including moths and butterflies) genitalia.

**Carbo animalis**: animal charcoal; substance made from charred corpses and ingested by humans to ease ailments ranging from plague buboes to homesickness, gangrene, syphilis, cough with greenish pus, frightful visions before rest, and old-age-induced blueness of skin.

**Cinnabar**: mercuric sulfide used in alchemy; also called vermillion.

**Chlorpromazine**: neuroleptic drug prescribed under the euphemism of "antipsychotic agent" to suppress the misunderstood cognitive-emotional expressions of those considered psychotic and try to "normalize" thought processes by slowing them. It is still unclear how chlorpromazine works, as its exact mechanism of action remains a mystery, but it is used nevertheless against those experiencing psychosis, especially those on the schizophrenia spectrum but also some bipolar patients and mal-behaving children. Also known to cause movement

problems, low blood pressure, increased weight, fatigue, tardive dys-
kinesia, neuroleptic malignant syndrome, low white blood cell count,
and more rapid onset of dementia and death.

**Choreomania**: Latin name used to describe the dancing madness,
dancing plague, dancing sickness, and St. Vitus' or St. John [the
Baptist]'s dance, which struck religious medieval Europe between the
fourteenth and seventeenth centuries. The name was coined by the
philosopher and alchemist Paracelsus and first diagnosed as a curse
sent by a saint. The mania caused the groups infected to dance errat-
ically to exhaustion, injury, and even death. Remedies included live
music and the color red, which also exacerbated and prolonged the
sufferers' frantic dancing.

**Cockroach**: many-legged mentor with the most humility, movement
intelligence, and tenacity, marking epochs of creative survival.

**Coywolf**: canid hybrid descendants of coyotes, wolves, and sometimes
dogs, uniting not only eastern and grey wolves with coyotes but also
the medieval penchant for hybrid creatures and mystical thinking
across continents.

**Croques-prépuces**: medieval surgeons experienced in tasting cir-
cumcised foreskins and hired by local priests to test the veracity of
the many Catholic relics purported to be the holy foreskin of Christ.
Another medieval theory proposed that when Christ ascended, his
foreskin was restored and widened to become Saturn's rings.

*Cum fossa et furca*: a medieval death sentence often pronounced for
convicted witches: "with drowning-pit and gallows;" also called trial
by drowning, this capital punishment was only abolished in the 1800s.

**Dance therapy**: rather than dance class or lessons with prescribed choreographies, creative authentic movement practices and dance healing explorations that enhance the integration of verbal and nonverbal understandings and the creation of meaningful cognitive-emotional expressions.

**Dancing sickness**: see Choreomania.

**Dead cart**: wheelbarrow into which the plague-dead were piled and transported during the medieval Black Death.

**Delirium tremens**: rapid onset of confusion, shaking, sweating, shivering, palpitating, trembling, or seizures that may be fatal. Often caused by withdrawal from substances, including psychiatric drugs such as benzodiazepines.

**DID**: dissociative identity "disorder." Multiplicity as a creative survival mechanism that lasts for life. Often involves a system with host(s), protector(s), gatekeeper(s), and more.

**Dulcification**: purifying alchemical process through which a caustic substance becomes less corrosive.

**Dysphoria**: from the Greek, meaning difficult to bear; an overwhelming or profound sense of unease.

**Echolalia**: repetition of vocalizations similar to ecopraxia, or the repetition of another's movements.

**Écraseur**: a surgical device bearing a chain or wire loop originally used to encircle and painfully strangle an ovary or polyp of the uterus until the tissue severed.

**Edulcoration**: the alchemical process of washing free from soluble impurities; to edulcate is to sweeten or purify.

**Effluvium**: invisible emanation, as from decay, as with miasma; odorous fumes.

**Emet**: Hebrew word for truth with the power to vivify formed from the first, middle, and last letters of the alphabet. These three letters, aleph, mem, and tav, compose the medieval mystic "seal of the Blessed Holy One" and are inscribed on the golem to make him self-animate.

**Emissary**: a part or representative part sent forth on a mission.

**Ether**: hypothetical fluid that transmits light in alchemical times.

**Euchlorine**: a bright green gas used in alchemy and believed to have been a chlorine-oxygen compound.

**Eugenics**: from the Greek "to come into being well;" a set of beliefs and practices to propagate those believed to have "good genes" and exclude, eventually eliminating, those deemed unworthy or inferior. Notoriously enforced under the Nazis and modeled after eugenic practices developed in the United States to prevent the mentally ill, women of color, inmates, the severely impoverished, and other undesirables from reproducing. Still used today to justify forced sterilizations, chemical castrations, lobotomies, and research aimed at identifying schizophrenia spectrum genetic markers to eliminate those affected in utero, as is now common practice in detecting and aborting fetuses with trisomy 21.

**Fleam**: also spelled phleam; medieval handheld venipucture device with a triangular blade often constructed from iron, thorns, stones, or teeth.

**Florid(ly psychotic)**: medical and therefore accidentally lovely term for the acute stages of psychosis.

**Flowers of antimony**: alchemical flowers are products of sublimation, in this case, antimony trioxide or antimony red.

**Friends of the Mentally Ill**: association that survives at Osawatomie State Hospital as one of the few vestiges of founding Quaker practices.

**Fulminating silver**: alchemical silver nitride, extremely explosive when dry.

**Genuflection**: the act of bowing on one knee in a gesture of respect used from medieval times in ritual Christian worship.

**Golem**: in early medieval writings as well as biblical psalms, literally any unformed, amorphous life. After Rabbi Loew, the mystically-invoked help or villain of the Jews under attack in Prague originally animated by any of the names of God inserted in the mouth or inscribed on the figure's clay or mud forehead.

**Hair mattress**: mattress filled with hair on which the mad were expected to sleep in the earliest madhouses, which functioned as cages for those deemed insane and amusement places for the neurotypical guests invited to watch the madmen and -women while enjoying snacks, prodding the patients with sticks, and experimenting with other diversions.

**Haloperidol**: neuroleptic drug or major tranquilizer marketed as a counteragent to psychosis and prescribed by psychiatric providers against schizophrenia spectrum and bipolar conditions. Suppresses cognitive processes and often causes uncontrollable drooling and other side effects such as weight gain, akathisia, dystonia, parkinsonism, hypotension, somnolence, and many more. Haloperidol also may be neurotoxic.

**Haruspex**: in ancient Rome, a seer who practiced divination by reading prophecies in entrails.

**Hemlock**: flowering plant often the poison of choice in ancient and medieval times, as ingestion leads to a harrowing death following stomach pain, vomiting, progressive paralysis, blindness, and asphyxia. See also poison parsley.

**Henbane**: the poison administered in ancient and medieval times to incite insanity. One of the poison plants containing belladonna alkaloids, along with mandrake, hemlock, yew extract, opium, and aconite.

**Hermes Trismegistus**: legendary ancestor of alchemy and its school of mysteries and syncretic face of multiple gods. One of the triumvirate deities called Hermes, for whom the alchemical Trismegistus or Thrice-Great is named, was an exile said to have given the Egyptians their laws and alphabet.

**Hippomane**: the Latin name *Hippomane mancinella* translates to "the little apple that makes horses mad." See manchineel. Also a fleshy black substance found on a newborn foal's forehead that was thought to be an aphrodisiac.

**Histrionic**: technically, dramatic or with deep affect, but also a term used to describe a personality perceived by medical practitioners as "disordered."

**Holy anorexic**: superhuman woman who showed she spoke for God in medieval tongues by proving she needed no nourishment but God's body, the host, thereby reclaiming the authority she should have been allowed to wield just by being. Described by Rudolph Bell in the study of medieval women mystics *Holy Anorexia*.

**Host**: the part of a system of multiples tasked with leading at the moment; the guest-giver; the organism on which others feed; the body (also of Christ).

**Human**: larger animal with fewer legs than cockroach.

**Human race**: misguided attempt to unite human people by denying the rights of those designated (by humans) as other species.

**Hypergraphia**: intensive drive or compulsion to practice writing in recognized verbal language or any other symbolic idioms, drawings, and so forth. Can be spurred by sources such as epilepsy and visions. Hildegard of Bingen also created a language of nouns drawn from a new alphabet, the *Litterae Ignotae*.

**Inchpin**: lower intestine of a deer from which the haruspex may divine.

**Katzenklavier**: medieval organ composed of cats. Cats are arranged according to notes on the keyboard approximated by their characteristic meow pitches. When an organ key is struck, the nail or needle driven through the mallet pricks the respective cat, who issues the musical note with her cry of pain.

**-kinesia**: suffix indicative of movement; also a motion sickness.

**Krokodil Gena**: Soviet stop motion animated film protagonist who, fittingly enough, works in a zoo as an attraction. Directed by Roman Abelevich Kachanov. In some scenes Krokodil Gena uses a bubble pipe.

**Laudanum**: any medicinal potion that features opium as the primary ingredient; often was available over the counter and administered to children.

**Mad-doctor**: the doctor-owner who presided over all the inmates interred at the madhouse.

**Madhouse**: enclosure used to lock away those deemed insane. The mad were kept in cages and viewed as a spectacle for visitors invited to amuse themselves by watching and provoking the prisoners by throwing stones through the enclosure bars, etc. The madhouse was the blueprint that became the modern psychiatric institution, with the mad renamed "patients" and the mad-doctors abbreviated to "doctors."

**Manchineel**: Hippomane mancinella, a flowering plant of the spurge family. One of the most toxic trees in the world, the bark and leaves cause blistering and death along with the fruit known as "the little apple of death." See Hippomane.

**Massicot flakes**: lead monoxide in a yellow powder form used in alchemy.

**#MeToo movement**: gender equity movement initiated by activist Tarana Burke in 2006 in The Bronx, New York, encouraging women to speak out against pervasive experiences of sexual abuse and violence.

**Mental Illness**: degrading designation used to separate and stigmatize many neurominorities, particularly those who use logic as a foreign language.

**Mercury**: used as an early neuroleptic that poisoned the insane in early madhouses into quiet and stillness. Exposure also causes pink, peeling skin, neuromuscular and neuerological disorders, tremors, memory loss, insomnia, pain, and death. **Mercury of Life** in alchemy is different: mercurius vitae.

**Methyl orange**: sodium *p*-Dimethylaminobenzenesulfonate in alchemy is orange and can fluctuate from red to yellow when PH is raised; methyl also appears in green and red spectrums, ranging from yellow always to blue-green or purple-red.

**Miasma**: any noxious vapor believed to emanate from organic matter in decay, either subtle in appearance or invisible.

**Million blue butterflies**: the parts of Lake Angela's illuminated soul.

**Neuroleptics**: chemical compounds more commonly known by the euphemism of "anti-psychotic agents." Prescribed to psychotic patients with the goal of normalizing psychomotor activity, these major tranquilizers work by inducing cognitive suppression, also causing apathy, decreased ranges of motion and emotion, parkinsonism, and a host of other serious side effects.

**Orbitoclast**: modified ice pick developed in 1948 to make lobotomies easier, outpatient procedures. The orbitoclast was hammered into the eye sockets, through the skull, and swung back and forth to destroy the brain's frontal lobes and separate them from the thalamus. The procedure was so violent that the metal orbitoclast sometimes broke while lodged in the patient's brain. The Nobel Prize was awarded for lobotomy in 1949.

**Padded room**: isolation chamber covered in padded surfaces where a patient can be kept to subdue or punish for undesirable behaviors. Still in use in most psychiatric institutions, both public and private, and often equipped with restraining devices as well.

**Perfect drink**: a reference to hemlock, opium, and wolfbane, a medieval concoction for an ecstatic death.

**Phosphorous**: term in alchemy for any phosphorescent substance; may appear in the form of flowers.

**Phrygian mode**: in the medieval context, spiritual musical or church mode in E, the third mode of the C Major scale that is actually a minor scale in quality. Pregnant women were prohibited from hearing this mode lest demons gain admittance to their bodies.

**Poison parsley**: ancient and medieval common name for hemlock because it resembles parsley except for the purple spots on the stem and the distinguishing odor. Also called devil's porridge, hemlock contains the poison coniine that leads to death upon ingestion after causing stomach pain, vomiting, progressive paralysis, blindness, and asphyxia.

**Prazosin**: alpha-blocker intended to lower blood pressure but used off-label to prevent nightmares in those suffering from post-traumatic stress symptoms.

**Products of conception**: new name for the embryo or fetus respectively when she dies in utero and is no longer medically considered to be a potential child nor a corpse.

**Psychosis**: an often solitary experience of a different reality for many mystics and visionaries; another way of knowing in which the reality of the psychotic thinker differs from that of neurotypical contemporaries. May present via visions or tactile, auditory, or other sensations, and may range from fear-inspiring to breathtaking and revolutionary.

**Punishment**: in this collection, as in medieval times, women mystics transformed the physical punishments meant to suppress their speech and test their devotions through bodily degradation into powerful assertions of their own spiritual authority. Medieval Veronica Giuliani was ordered by the Jesuit superior who investigated whether she was a saint or a witch to scour a disused cell floor with only her tongue; she swallowed spiders, dirt, and cobwebs with ardor. Angela of Foligno, mystic love poet who came to know "the visions and the words" and saw God "more ineffably, more darkly," swallowed the scabs and pus she cleaned from a leper's body, and Birgitta of Sweden swallowed Christ's foreskin as host in a vision that transformed her.

**Rack**: medieval torture or martyrdom device that dislodges the victim's joints by pulling her apart.

**Reality therapy**: outmoded and ineffective approach to therapy in which psychologists discount and contradict the patients' experiences.

**Remedium**: medieval Latin name for any kind of medicinal cure or relief, ideally a panacea but more often a remedy for an ailment perceived to be minor.

**Rose vitriol**: cobalt (II) sulfate in alchemy, used because vitriol could corrode almost all substances except gold.

**Saffron of Mars**: alchemical yellow from an iron compound.

**Saturn cure**: any lead compound used as a cure in alchemy; also influence from the heavenly body.

**Schizophrenia spectrum**: a spectrum of creative cognitive-emotional differences characterized by more vast associative leaps than are neurotypical and by intensive metaphor. Includes schizoaffective conditions.

**Scivias**: Latin title of Hildegard of Bingen's most renowned medieval work. Literally "know the ways," the work details powerful ways of knowing other-than-human verbal language through depictions of her visions imparted by the voice of Heaven and her detailed illuminations divided in three parts for the Trinity. Part three is as long as parts one and two combined, as in this collection. God commanded that *Scivias* be transcribed in verbal language. Retrospective diagnoses of epilepsy do not invalidate the meanings of Hildegard's visions and voices or poetic, scientific, and musical innovations, just as contemporary diagnoses of schizoaffective thinking and multiplicity do not alter the meaningful depths, value, and beauty of the unusual metaphors and imagery present in poetry.

**Silence**: a realm of unspoken languages, similar to darkness in its infinite depths of unshaped meanings; one of the liminalities in which meanings are made.

**Sister Barb**: commander and creator of the term unemployed angels; a long-time hermitess of the Franciscan order in the northern United States.

**Sociopathy**: at The Asylum for the Insane in rural Kansas from which Part II of this volume derives, this term was used interchangeably with psychopathy to describe those patients convicted of major crimes or those seemingly devoid of empathy. Term also used as an insult, similar to the misuse of the label schizophrenia.

**Strepitus**: literally, a sonorous or loud noise; the loud noise, such as a stamping of the feet, that ends the western Christian Tenebrae service in total darkness after the candles are extinguished. Held in Latin Catholic Churches three days before the day of resurrection.

**Sugar of lead**: lead acetate used in alchemy.

**Sulfur**: also sulphur; in alchemy, believed to be the source or cause of inflammability and fiery yellow color and odor; in Catholicism, bears parallel reference to the odor and color of hellfire.

**Tenebrae**: in Latin, darkness; a medieval religious service that lingers during which all candles gradually are extinguished and the silence is interrupted by a final loud noise, or strepitus.

**Tranquilizers**: any of the drugs designed and administered or injected to cause sedation; generally divided into major and minor tranquilizers. Though many can be fatal, the harshest, the major tranquilizers, often are repeatedly administered to those who experience psychosis. Tranquilizing plant alkaloids also can be poisonous in certain doses.

**Transorbital lobotomy orbitoclast**: a modified ice pick developed by an American physicist in the mid-20th century as a quick way to lobotomize patients in an outpatient process by stabbing the metal pick in and out of the brain through the eye sockets, destroying tissues and connections in the prefrontal cortex and at times killing the patient.

**Treppaning**: the act of trepanation is a boring or scraping of a hole in the skull according to the ancient and medieval surgical procedures to exorcise or free the demons from one deemed to be possessed, ill, or behaving oddly. In other contexts, the hole serves as a portal for spiritual communication.

**Triangle**: the most frightening sign and a favorite of Catholics.

**Tuberculosis cottage**: building on Osawatomie asylum grounds where the tubercular insane were confined. In a derelict state but not yet burned nor torn down, the cottage stands because the tubercular particles were believed to linger for fifty years after the last patient's departing breath. The institution's grounds also house a school, prison, morgue, and graveyards, some overt and some hidden beneath other sites.

**Tunnels**: subterranean chambers under Osawatomie hospital grounds where patients were chained during "episodes" or made to walk from one building to another in darkness because it was believed that the insane would react with heightened madness if exposed to daylight.

**Vermillion**: alternative name for cinnabar used in alchemical processes; mercuric sulfide.

**Votive**: offering in fulfilment of a vow; a candle symbolizing such dedication or offering associated with Catholicism.

**White flux**: the boiling wound of a tree stressed with heat in which microorganisms ferment sap in cuts and scabs, causing white froth and pleasantly odoriferous gas. Also an alchemical designation.

**Witch pricking**: professional specialization of witch hunters who searched a suspected woman's naked body for marks of Satan, such as freckles, pocks, scars, or moles. The hunter stabbed the spot with a specially-designed, long, retracting needle. If the spot did not bleed, the woman was proven guilty and killed. Sometimes victims were pricked repeatedly until the hunter could locate a mark, visible or not, that did not bleed, thereby condemning the suspect to a burning death.

**Woodbine**: twining Eurasian plant cut on the waxing moon and wound into a hoop as protection against the plague and to cure ill children who passed through three times.

**Yarrow**: among the oldest medicinal herbs, from *hieros*, or sacred; kept under the pillow or burned as protection against the black death; used as an antispasmodic and cure for almost every other ailment; flowering herb with bitter taste, often used by healing women for women.

LAKE ANGELA is a poet, translator, and dancer-choreographer who creates at the confluence of verbal language and movement. Her other books of poetry include *Organblooms* and *Words for the Dead* from FutureCycle Press. She holds a PhD in the intersemiotic translation of Austrian Expressionist poetry into dance and has her MFA in poetry. Lake is an editor for the multilingual arts journal *Punt Volat*. She is a medieval mystic, beguine, and nonhuman creature. As director of the poetry-dance group Companyia Lake Angela, she presents the value of schizophrenia spectrum creativity. She welcomes visitors and collaborators at www.lakeangeladance.com.